Convalesce

Enne Zale

Convalesce

atmosphere press

Dedicated to my parents and to my love,
to whom this book is a collection of my confessions.

My poetry has no chronological order,
The bitter moments intertwine with the sweet ones
Because like life
You do not solely have good periods and bad ones.
No you do not
The struggle of fighting what lingers in the depths
Of your mind is constant.
There are times healing feels complete
Then the next hour the walls close in
And the invisible hands touch your body once more.
There are moments where your emotions flare
And you cannot control the tears from running
Or the laughs from escaping the
Twisted curl of your lips.
The book may feel scattered
But it's a reflection of my inner soul.
It is the book of a bubble-wrapped girl
Who was unboxed too early.
A toy who was given to the wrong set of hands
Mistreated and then deployed.
It's the story of a woman who learned to tolerate
Her counterparts
Learned to love again
And who struggles to enjoy the present
Because her past refuses to loosen the grasp
Around her neck.

The world is full of shades of grey both light and dark.
I remember a time when vivid hues danced through the layers
    of my reality.
But a shadow caught my attention,
And against my better judgment I chased after it.
For a moment we embraced and you provided the contrast I
needed to be more radiant.
With every breath we took together you made me- fade?
My innocence and "rosy lenses" turned dull.
Like the night you engulfed me and disappeared.
I want someone to bring color into my life once more,
But I also want my world to remain like this.

Give me warmth and comfort me.
The scars on my skin tingle more profoundly near the heat.
I've been burnt many times,
Yet the flickering flames still entrance me.

Look but don't touch.

Love without lust.

But who am I to you?
What am I to you?

Those words linger,
Eating away at my mind.
Ships float away without their anchors.
Both meant to occupy the same space yet don't belong
together.
One stays grounded while the other drifts.

I refuse to be the drifting boat
So I throw myself into the ocean to meet you in the depths.
The water is cold and vast.
It's full of wondrous creatures
Yet none are comparable.

But what am I to you?
Who am I to you?

Your touch healed my scars
And your words swept away my insecurities.
How I wish you could have stayed forever.
But that would be selfish.

Your arms still hold me close
And your eyes still look into my soul.
How I wish you had stayed a little longer.
Thank you for healing my scars..

I may not appear to be strong
But I refuse to be weak.
Those around me struggle to hold on
Against the unrelenting winds…
Not I.

I let go
And disappear into the horizon.
Take me where you must,
Let them think I have no perseverance to hold on.
But know I've accepted who I'm supposed to be.
I'm a sinner masked as a survivor.
It's not my place to have
expectations for others
Some must stay and fight
Not I.

I will venture forth
To face the force that struggles to push me back.
I Have fear of the uncertainty,
But I refuse to be weak.

I like it rough.

Not because it's a kink

But I've been used so many times

I can no longer feel the presence of a soft touch.

If it can't be confused for assault

You aren't loving me right.

I say that because it's what I've been taught by every man I've
    opened my legs for.

Or should I say for every time my legs were opened by a man.

Don't be gentle with me

I need to know you're here-

That you're touching me

And these damaged goods I call my body.

Harder- Because the shots of pain

Can be mistaken for pleasure.

I like it rough

For my body is too numb

To recognize the delicate hands

That should have touched me first.

A Man's Best Friend-
I find my way to you in every lifetime
Solely to stand by your side.
Hold me and I'll protect you.
Say you love me and I'll die for you.
Neglect me and I'll wait for you to return.

Even if I must wait for our next lives.

I notice your quirks and adore your entirety.
I know the demons that linger in your heart.
Even if to you I am inconsequential,
I'm infatuated and will love you regardless.

Unrequited love appears to have turned me into a dog.

She looked defeated
The way her eyes drift into the distance
And her hands hang from the bed.

Get up.

A small voice begins to clammer in the back of her mind.
Scared, if she doesn't lift herself now she may never rise again.

Get up.

A little louder now.
A wince for how heavy her body feels
Magnetically pulled back to the ground.

Get up.

Her head finally lifts from between her arms
But then sinks back into their warmth.

Stay down.

Because getting up would mean she'd have to try one more.

Dazzled by a fake smile
To get you in the mood.

Can you see the beast inside?

Lower your defenses
I'll pull you in like the tide.

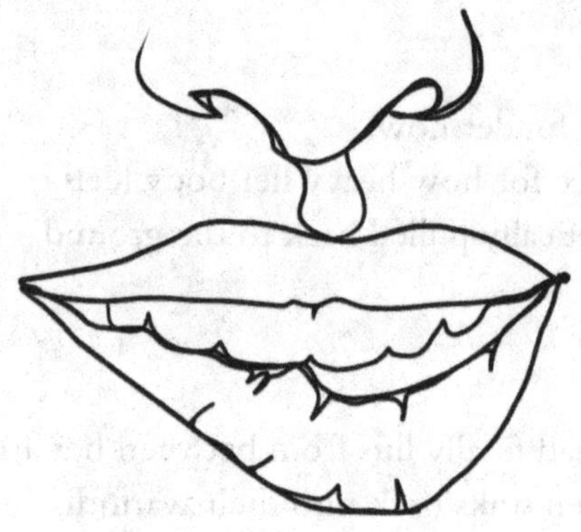

The saddest truth is accepting
You can no longer light up a room with your smile
When you can't even find a spark to continue.

"You're silly, stay that way."
I smile now
Not for bliss…
But because I won't let you take that away too

I'm not broken.
I've simply found peace.
It's ok not to smile
As it's ok to feel no pain.
I'd rather exist
So that one day… those feelings may return.

I'd rather be called a careless idiot
Than the word that takes away all control.
Hold me accountable for what happened
So that the shame lessens.
A person of opportunity.

A victim.

I've changed.
I used to be strong and bold.
Reality says I was neither.
I was ignorant and gullible.

The adversity has shaped me,
And I can't fit into the skin
I once wore it proudly.

Sometimes I wonder
What if i'm not strong enough
My head rises
Chin up and shoulders back.

Whether or not it is irrelevant.

I can't afford not to be.

The hardest part
Is accepting it was fake
And hoping parts of it were real...

For every fault I found
You saw beauty.
With every insecurity,
You saw a duty
To show me how precious I am.

-    A good father

An instant connection- lost.
Let it die,
Because it is easier.

Easier than learning to love again.

AUG 20

"You belong to me."
Sweet words now sound bitter.
Close my eyes
While you search for someone better.
Disappear for some days
And leave me here broken.
I come to find
That I was just a token.

Death knocked on my door today
To see the state I was in.
When I opened up
Death closed the door on me
And said
"There is no living here
I was mistaken."

Shatter the remains of my heart
So that the pieces can fit in yours.
Let my soul fill the holes remaining
Can two broken people share a heart?

Perhaps if fear didn't grasp our necks
And salty tears didn't stain our faces.
If we had met a little sooner
We could have loved a little harder.

Beautiful stranger
Save our dance for another life.

The clock spins too quickly
When I beam with excitement.

The clock has sluggish movements
When boredom seeps in.

The clock keeps ticking
When the beating of my heart stops.

Time always seems to oppose us.

The girl before

Her heart would've melted
With the sweet words you speak.

The girl now

Her heart grows numb
With the empty words you speak too easily.

Hearing isn't feeling.

I lost my heart
Suddenly everyone is after the hidden treasure.
It's funny how things aren't valued until they vanish.
Pirates always hoard the rarest oddities.
But a girl with a heart made of gold was the hidden gem they
    missed.

A pretty face will take you places.
A broken heart will create new faces.
I'll repeat your sins and play with cases.
Turn this into a daily basis.

The phrase goes
I didn't want to hurt you.

But in reality
I don't want to hurt again.

Her future involved

Little feet & clingy hands.

Nights of cuddling and

Whispers of "I love you."

People don't simply vanish.

It takes time for a soul to corrupt
And silent cries to go unnoticed.

You killed me.

She's the kind of person
Who anyone can be friends with
But it's hard to be special to her...

She's the kind of person
Who thinks anyone is replaceable
Because everyone is replaceable.

Good girls with bad habits-
***Bad girls with good habits

Not the way I intended
But mistakes happen.
So spice this shit up.

A smile not meant for me
Never looked so beautiful.
The thud in my chest
Never felt more precious.

It wasn't til I walked away

You said the words "you need to stay."

It's hard to love someone who left

Because if they can do it once

They're sure to walk away again.

Learning to trust
Is finding warmth in a flame
And hoping you don't get burned.

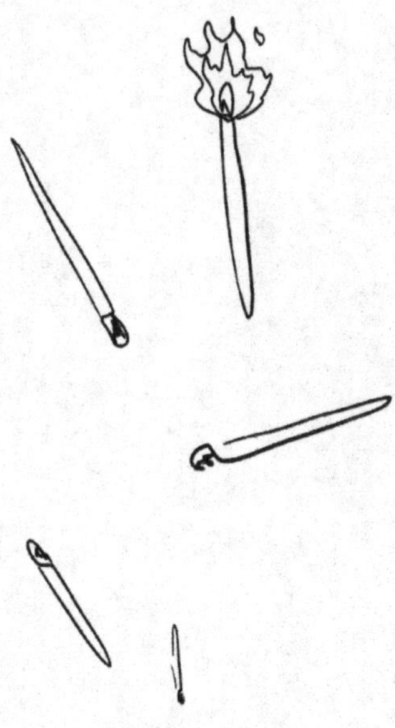

I hid my heart
And you sought to find it.

Stayed away and came back to
Many lies and hidden truths.
Can't be with or without you.

No one can
break
or put my heart back
together
better than you

Falling taught me something

They'll only try to catch you
After you get up.

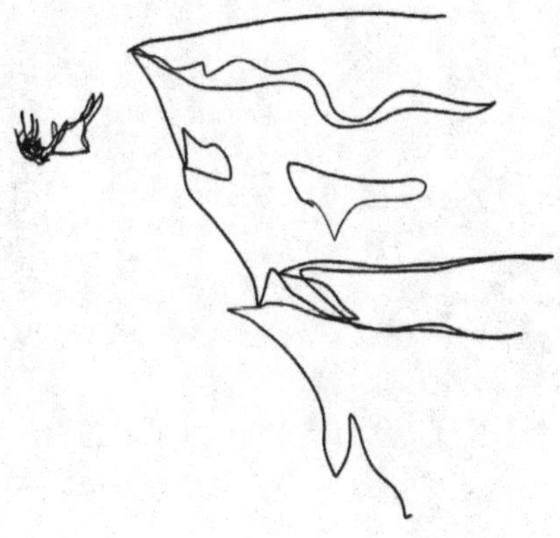

Memories turn to nightmares

And innocence is lost.

I'm surrounded by many
Yet I've never felt so lonely.
No more…
I'm done.

How is it I can write a million poems,

But I lose my words
Speaking to you.

In trying not to love you
I've become versatile in every aspect of life.
It seems I've become capable of anything
Everything except forgetting you.

Listen to a sad melody in times of despair.

I want to feel this pain.
Let it simmer and sting.

Anything is better than being empty.

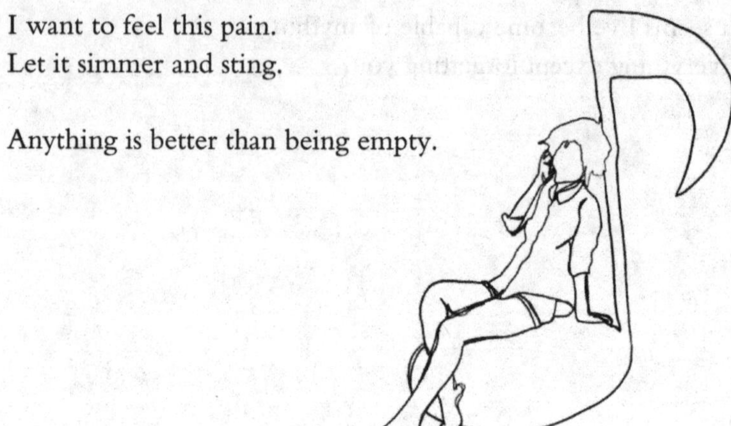

Put some miles between us
Or pull me closer.

Let our promise fade
Or say I love you.

Distance disturbs me
So does your ignorance.

The easiest part
Was accepting
You'd never come.

The hardest part
Was experiencing it.

Remind me of my failures
And show me the worthlessness of my existence.
Forget me so that I may fade peacefully.

Truth is

I'm doing fine.
You're never on my mind.
There are times when shit looks bleak
But I'll never be fucking weak.

Truth is

I don't think of you anymore.
I enjoy being a whore.
I'd like to say at least I tried.

Truth is I lied.

Missing you is kind of unbearable.
So I close my eyes and revisit every moment
Spent with you
My heart races
I can't tell if it's fear, pain, or bliss…
I take this pen and scribble out the faces
Of every person who plays a part in my story.
No one exists anymore.
My memories are full of blank faces
With scribbles that make my memories numb.
I realize emotions come from experience
Who knew removing people from my moments turns my
     world grey.
So many scribbles.

Who are you again?

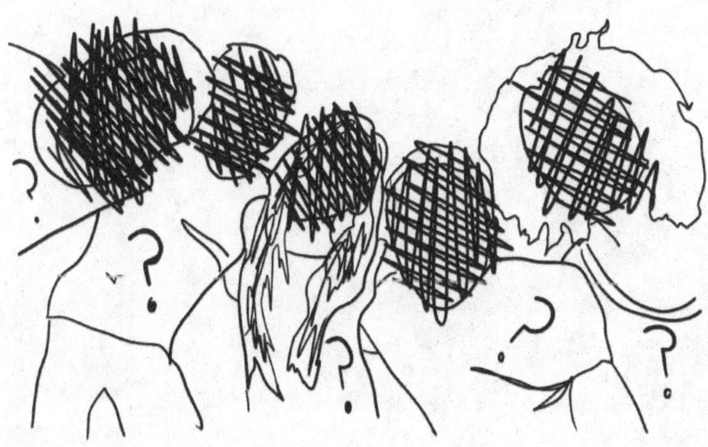

You can inspire
But you can't install hope.
Without a cause
Motivation is pointless.

If it's you

I'd do it all again.
I'll do it all again.

The truth is

I'm ashamed of my life

And the emptiness imprinted.

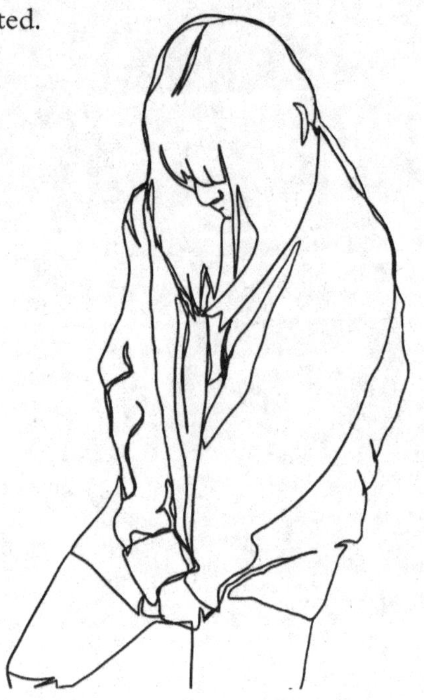

I'm ashamed of my life

At least

Nightmares

Induce

fear.

Live a long
Happy
Beautiful
Life without me.

In a world full of copies
I'm happy to have myself.

I don't feel anything anymore.

I'm content with this tranquility.

Feeling too much
Or feeling nothing at all.
It's all beautiful.

Bury a friend.

It's easier than helping her.

She dug herself into a hole.

Bury a friend.

Don't say dreams don't come true.
Nightmares are dreams too.

My brain functions differently from a normal person.

Don't ask me my reasons because you'd never understand.

Don't question my actions because they are who I am.

Why reminisce on bad times

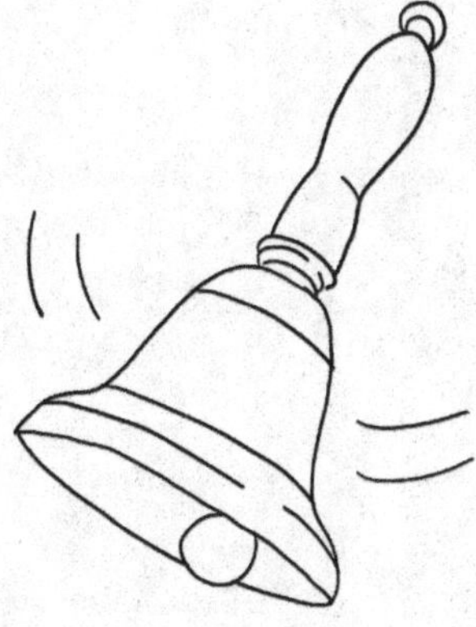

When the good memories ring louder?

I'd rather suffer
From a broken heart
Than an empty one.

When I chose to walk
It wasn't to get away from you,
It was for the chase.

When I said those words
It wasn't supposed to be true,
I wanted you to fight.

When I stayed away
It wasn't to hide from you,
I wanted you to find me.

I write to forget
With every stroke of the wrist
My memories transfer
To the words on the page
And allow me to survive another day

Ask me of my past but I can't remember
Read my life on paper
And I'll surely speak to you.

Fake flowers last longer than real ones.

Guess the same can be said about people.

Trudging with a broken heart
The pieces got lost in the shadows.
Now I steal hearts
But nothing seems to fit the void quite right.

Beat…
Heart–beat?

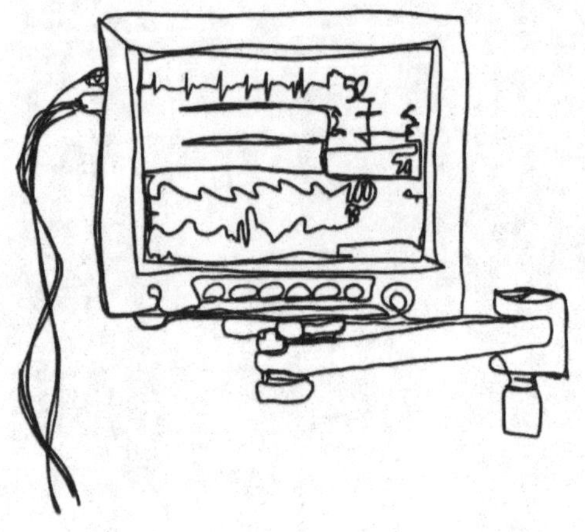

"You are what you eat"
I've had a million sweets
Tell me why I'm still bitter.

I'm a skeptic of
Beautiful things.

Every piece of pain
Deserves its own audience.

A man of greatness

Little words
Great charity.

A mentor,
A friend.

Rest in peace

Even though it was only for a day
You showed me what's possible
I would have liked it to be you
But you showed me what's possible
Even though it was only for a day.

After you

I don't love as deeply
Or speak as softly.
I accept being alone
And having a voice
Over wearing a filter
To please another.

I thought about it
And I don't hate you.
I could never hate someone who made me happy.

I thought about it
And we no longer click.
I can't stand by someone who makes me feel empty.

I thought about it
And I hope you're happy
I wish the best for someone who once made me happy.

I fell in love with someone
That told me I was enough.

I fell down when he showed me I wasn't.

You were the ocean and

I was trying to explore space.

I can do this
Even if you're not here.

My behavior was unnecessary
Because to him nothing was wrong.

You can pour your heart out only so many times.

1: What did you accomplish by telling him?
2: Well now he's aware.
1: And what does that change
2: I'm not a hypocrite.
1: …

I'm icing my heart
Surrounding it in flames.
It's truly an art
The way I ignore my pain.

It seems my greatest desires are never tangible,

Like you.

Let me go numb.
If I don't feel
It's not real.

It's true what they say

Only the ignorant ones get played.

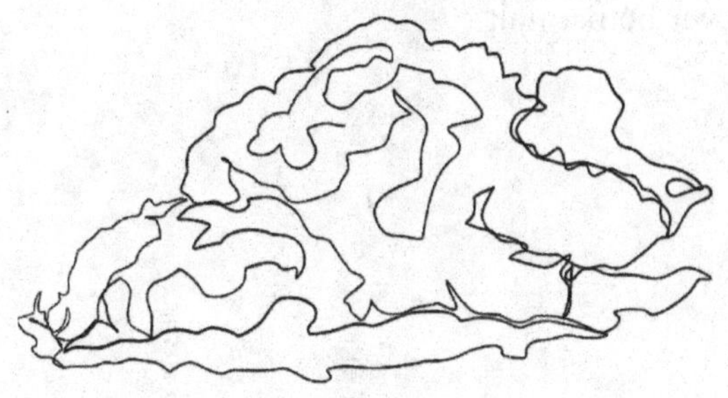

Do you still think of me?

"I would be a cloud if just to be present."

I want you to know me.

But it'll never be natural.

Fragile.
If I leave it alone
It should go away.
But if you ignore his tone
You won't know what to say.

Any plant left unattended will wither.
The roots desperately seek for familiarity.
These poisonous words seem so bitter
With thunder where do you find clarity?

Listen to the silent sobs of falling rain.
Each drop groans with fears
Helplessly watching the train
Approaching a breakdown in tears.

Yet it can regrow
But it'll never be the same
This pain you bestow,
A never ending game.

I need to stop loving you
Before I start hating you.

You're hella stupid
Wish you knew
I'll spend some time
Missing you

Reality follows into my slumber

With weeks passing I've lost count of the number

Nights full of seeing ghost and pale faces

Memories sting leaving harsh traces

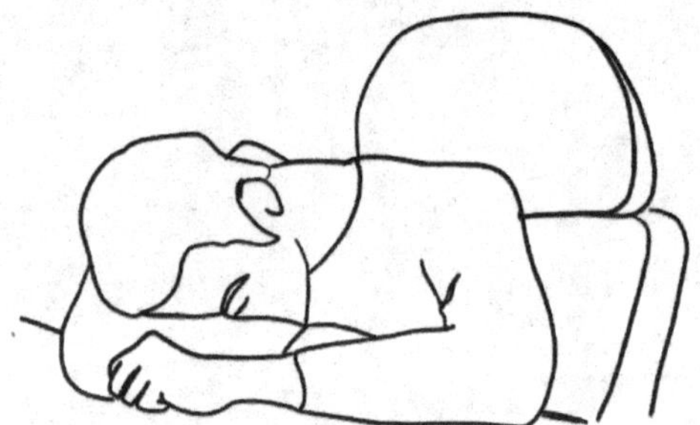

The fear of not reaching you

Outweighed the fear of falling

Two minutes of bliss with you
Is worth a lifetime of agony.
There is no greater pain
Than being apart.
There is no bigger blessing
Than seeing you smile.

Standing there I was

With you.

The person I thought would never leave.

Suddenly I could have

Everything I ever wanted.

So I walked the other direction.

I think of you often.

Because I never understood you

I fantasized a person

And pretended it was true.

I lie awake often

Because I always knew–

To love the mystery more than the guy

Enough to fall for his lies.

All that was left was for me to say goodbye.

If you were to die
So would I.

So let me continue to stay by your side.

He was a comet–
When you hold onto people
Like that for too long…
You're going to burn.

If you ever try to leave me behind like that again

And succeed…

Understand you're not taking away one

But two lives.

I would have preferred
It'd gone a different way.

But I'm honestly
Not surprised you ran away.

She was like a black widow

Beautifully discreet

Toxic
            &
                    Tranquil.

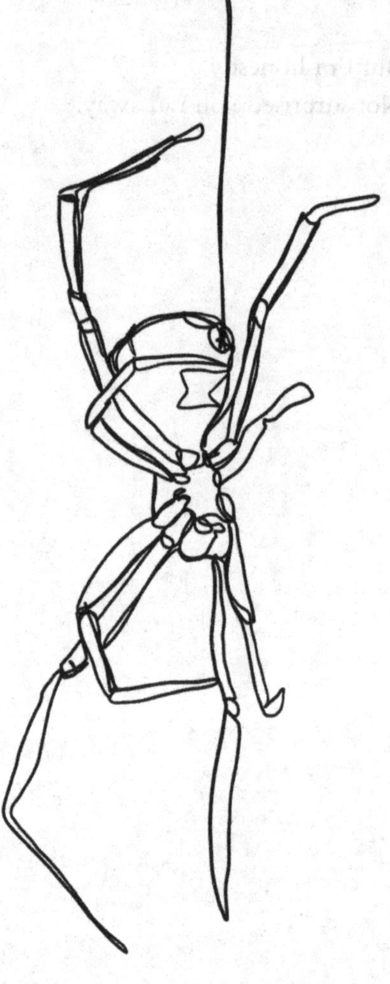

She simply wished to be held.

Wondering hands and soft words

Masked the coaxing of a lamb.

Hold her throat so she doesn't speak.

Kiss her skin so she doesn't think.

The mask falls off yet trapped in a scam

With every plea the fainter her "no's

She simply wished to never be touched again.

Who knew
I was one heartbreak away
From feeling nothing at all.

Was I so easy to forget?

You took chapters to explain in my story.

To you

I was simply a cameo.

"I'm sorry."

These words leave a sour taste in my mouth- ending in
bitterness beyond the lips.

I did nothing wrong.

But I'd rather say these words than lose you.

And yes
You're forgiven.

You lost the right to speak
To me the moment your
Lust outweighed
Our friendship.

Chills run and the sky is bleak
Solemn eyes that scream for "help!"
Intensifies with a belt.

Look at me but you'll never find
Any trace of a wholesome mind.

The poor child suffered hideous crimes
He came to hurt them one last time.

   -    *A friend who did not make it.*

Kiss me.

Let the silence say the words we dare not speak.
Allow the tingles to travel and caress our bodies.
Let the rhythm of our hearts synchronize
While I listen to the soft
Melody of your breathing.

Kiss me.

For this is but a moment that ends in silence.

The word relationship scares the me,
Commitment and vulnerability… crazy.
I doubt you'll love me forever
And I doubt I won't run away.
But the love in your eyes
Tell me it's ok to stay like this with you.

At least for now.

Grass blades are very much like people.

In a group they seem harmless.

But after rolling in the field

You find that your skin burns.

Invisible cuts cover your body.

Now add some salt.

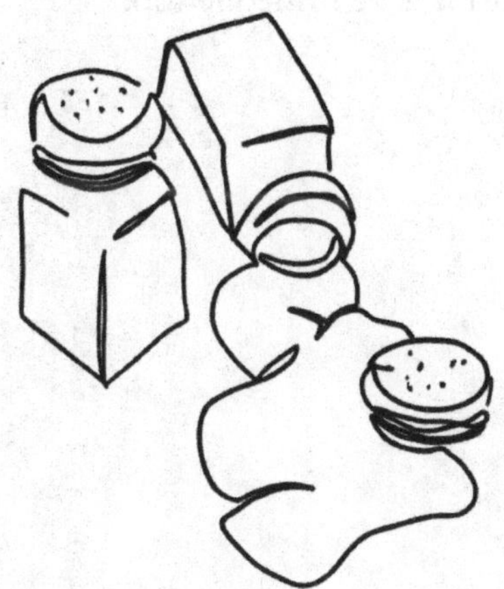

I simply wish for empty company

Sit in a public place to see happy faces

And to hear eager voices

Life gets lonesome,

The hole in my chest

Fills with hope.

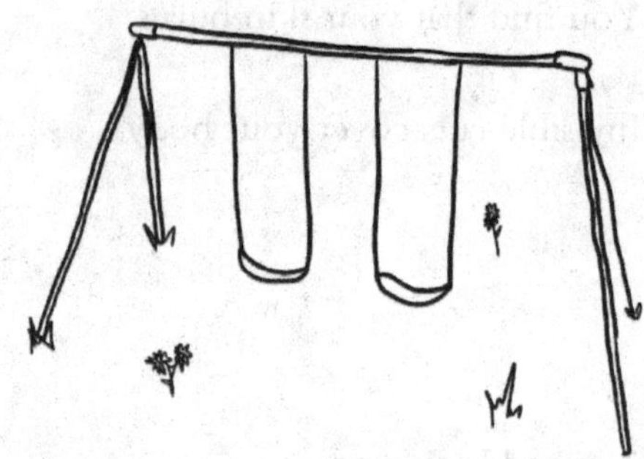

Maybe not today,

But I'll have someone too.

It takes a special kind of girl
To seduce the strongest of men.
By simply existing.

I tend to have that effect on people.

I simply give off a vibe
That makes great people
Succumb to sexual desires.

The human version of a succubus,
The stupid curse of a "minx."

"L" stands for "love"

But

It also stands for "lonely"

Which

Can lead to "lust"

"L" stands for "lament"

Why are you here?

If I say, you won't like my answer.

Why are you here?!

Let's just say there was a small tragedy. A promise. Followed by
    a life-sentence.

A normal day of simplicity

Interrupted with a shift in the atmosphere.

Who allowed one man to cause so much fear?

A certain flare in the eyes that makes my blood run cold.

The glare of sharks…

Misty pupils that whisper lusters desires.

The small remarks…

Playful words that sends trembles down every nerve.

Who allowed one man to cause so much fear?

A normal day of simplicity-

Until this became my reality.

A shadow swallows away the
Warmth and comfort
The pillar looks lonely from here
But all I see is you.
And I wonder, why can't you see me?
I stand silently in the cold
Waiting for you to let me in.

I speak no words in the daylight
Because I want our bond to
Transcend simple interactions of camaraderies.
The melody of heartbreak sounds
Bittersweet coming from you.
And I wonder, why can't you hear me?
I stand in the hell fires waiting
For you to put me out.

A small whimper of loneliness
Escapes my lips.
You wish for another while I wish for you.
You see another while I blindly choose you.
You listen to every word but "I love you"

It's not for everyone
But don't be so condescending.
I can't imagine your boring existence
For you to find this entertaining.

When I was broken
You told me my life had meaning.
Your love had meaning to me
And that was tossed away.
What does that say about me and my life?

I don't know.
You do the right thing
Yet manage to fuck up the right thing.

To venture my mind
And not my body
I wonder what that feels like

You think it's sweet til
You bite into it.

Then you realize you chose the wrong candy.

What's the point of even trying

When my heart is slowly dying?

Grip the delicate flesh
And hope I don't bruise so easily.
Taunt the state of mind
And hope my words don't slip so carelessly
The memories fade
And the scars linger.
They say my pain is fake
Then so are the bruises under my t-shirt.

Someday a warmth will fester from my chest

My resolve is that this is only temporary.

Tender eyes
Broken hearts
Fucked up feelings
Messed up charts-
Charts that tell you how you're feeling
By someone who DON'T know how you're feeling
Trynna act like what you're feeling
Ain't right in the head.
But in your heart
Made of shattered pieces
You picked one up to find your reason-
Reason being you ain't dead.

You ain't dead.

Tender eyes
Broken hearts
Fucked up feelings
Reminding you that you ain't dead.

Even if you wish you were.

She simply wished to be found.
Recognized as she was
Something more than yesterday
A little less than tomorrow.

You promised you loved me,
But you did not want me.

How could that play out?

I told you I'd wait here.
But didn't know that being near

Had a way of tearing me down.

To stay but at a distance,
To love without existence,

Help me find a way out.

A resting hand on my cheek
A steady gaze in my soul.
I simply wanted to hold you tight
And never have to let go.

But as you know it's not that easy
To love someone who's always thinking
Our love's destruction grows intangible.

Indefinitely,

You may never be just friends with someone you love.

Fire burns
But that's not
What killed
Our desire.

Without turning around I can tell

It's you

From the shift in the air

When you appear.

No one feels the same.

Never understood how others can

Tell me to seek company

After you're gone.

No one feels the same.

Staying here with you

What will that change?

You are scared to love

I am scared to be unloved.

To coexist is to hurt.

The rarest tragedy is two hearts who can't compromise.

Fell in love
Might delete later.

He fucked up
He'll regret it later..

131

Disappearing would be too kind
Along with the agony of a throbbing heart.
Let my fingers dance within your veins and watch closely
As you are now tamed.

A man that can't be left behind
A girl whose heart was undermined
Two broken hearts craving comfort
Stand aside and choose to suffer

Suffer tears
Or suffer losses.

Wishing for the other to compromise
Yet analyze
And choose to hide
And severe ties
From each other
Neither can leave the other behind
But in doing so ended up farther apart.

Vibrant hues of every shade
Something sweet begins to decay.

Drawn to her for her spectrum
They never knew why she left 'em.

Pastels and reds, arrays of blue
If only he had loved her too.

Stained with pain of rejection
Different greys took over her complexion.

She got greedy and absorbed every color
Now she wears black and her insecurities wrapped around her
    collar.

Everyone has their own path to follow
Some collectively gather on the roads
While others pave their own.
Where does one go
When they were dropped in the middle of nowhere?
How does one pave
When they have no drive to start
And too many problems to bear?

Younger me
Would've killed
For what I'm walking away from now.

Don't disappear.

How does one hold onto something fading
Someone whose time is long overdue?

Don't disappear.

Even though it seems we don't belong.

Don't disappear.

I'll defy the universe to be beside you.

Don't disap

Our desire for what we wanted
Was greater than
 Our desire for each other.

Lack of compromise killed us.

Blades of green seem redundant
Til the heart's a respondent.
A cut that turns
To an itch that burns
To love again,
I'm a bit reluctant.

I hate it when
They ask me how I'm doing.

Cuz I'm always
Gonna say I'm doing alright.

I hate it when
They tell me what they're doing.

Gotta act
Like I'm interested in their life.

Why is it that
Doing the right thing
Hurts just as much
As doing the wrong thing?

If not worse...

You did nothing wrong
And gave him everything.
But if you choose a small cup
It is bound to overflow.

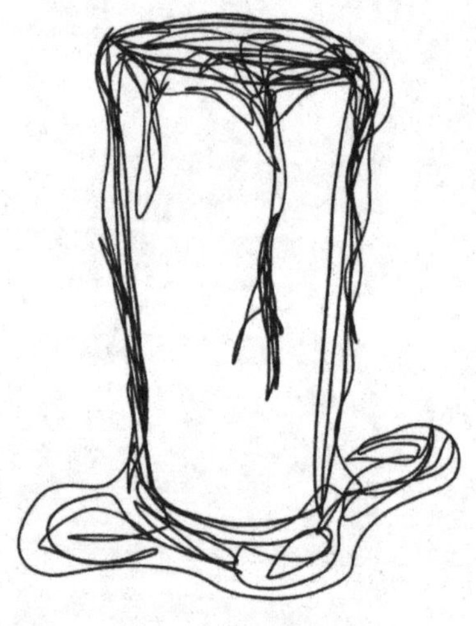

My soul's engulfed in fire.
My heart beats in a frenzy
Wishing to be liberated from the flames.

My veins throb.

My limbs aching

To cling or claw at anyone for comfort.

Don't venture near.
A single brushing of my skin
Signifies you will burn too.

As long as the stars remain overhead
I'll treasure the fragments left on the bed.
Treasure?
Such a precious way of saying you stole
My virtue and left me for dead.
Left me dead- inside.
I look to the girl who watched stars
And shrivel to know you are down there
Watching them with her.
I like stars
Because it shows glistening fragments
Moments of what could have been.
It's the light forever fleeting my body
Knowing she is dead because of the way
You treated her in bed.
The subtle tensions of loneliness
To know that both girls who look up at the stars are me.

From before and after you stole my virtue.

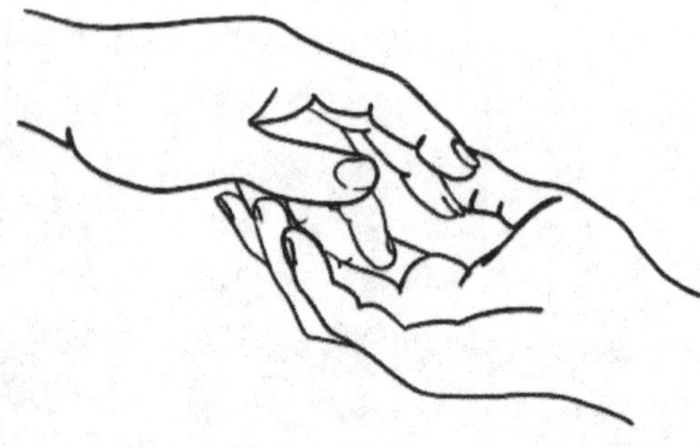

Run but I won't chase you

You'll walk away?

Watch me move on.

I don't fight for people to be in my life–

People fight to be in it.

I won't cry over a boy who couldn't stay.

But you'll cry for the good woman that left.

Replicate a feeling
Before they catch on.

The girl who chose to
Suffocate on toxins
Before he moved on
Now sits feeling boxed in
Since she lost their bond.
Call the next of kin
Because she is gone.

Replicate a feeling
Before they catch on.

Almost had something real
But it faded away.
There's nothing to say…
You'll be okay.

There are times
When being loved lets you reach a sense of euphoria
Where the hurt disappears because you were enough
For someone to love.

But in the end
The ones you choose always seem to be leaving
Could it be due to your insecurities
Or your inability to submit?
Or that they lacked the maturity
To admit they could not commit.

In the beginning we were a team.
Best friends forever or so it would seem.
You called me the glue that held us together.
And said without me y'all wouldn't last past
September

There was a party
Apart we were hardly.

When apart we'd call for hours
And feel empowered.

Each of us holding a special role
But a day without me took a toll.

Everyday use to be an adventure
Now I can hardly remember.

The last call, the last text
Eventually y'all confessed.

One plus one doesn't equal three.
The two of you together no longer includes me.

You were a warm summer breeze
And I, a cold winter tease.
As we embraced we ignored the tension
A storm brewed without comprehension.

Lightning felt like sparks flying
And thunder is mistaken for a beating heart.

The chaos was rationalized
Til it left us hospitalized.
When opposite fronts meet
They're bound to feel the heat.
When opposite fronts intertwine,
One will always be undermined.

Maybe it's time
I start saying goodbye
And wander
Through panes of unfamiliar faces

In a life of no guarantees
Full of false appearances
Constant broken promises
And people with no tolerances.

I met a boy who wasn't entitled
To the illusions of paradise.

He now lives in the moment
An adrenaline junkie is what was chosen
Because he was once so broken
And can't imagine his life not in motion.

The boy who liked red
Never looked so good feeling blue.

For someone who's lovely
Disappearing is the scariest thing
Now I purposely choose to go off the grid.
So that my solitude is peaceful
And my pride is intact.

A heart that holds toxins
Can only inflict grief and ecstasy

The symptoms include feelings of highs, sweaty hands, an
increased heartbeat, and pure infatuation.

Masked by love,
The victims endure it all
Until they are left broken and unsteady

They gave you their heart too easily...
Full of toxins and games.
You took it too quickly...
Now you fall limp and tamed.

If the only relief
From the aching,
This aching- resolves in losing you…

Let it burn.

They say the only relief
From anguish,
This anguish- is letting you go…

Let it simmer.

Although you don't understand,
I'd rather drown beside you
Than survive without you.

I love you
Because I love to be bothered.

Lone survivor.

Was winning worth your new found spoils of the vast abyss?
The abyss known as loneliness and empty cradles.

An empty cradle that could have echoed with the cries- the soft
    wailing of a newborn child.
A child you felt was unnecessary.

Lone survivor.

Was winning worth your new found spoils of the vast abyss?
The abyss known as loneliness and a broken childhood.

A childhood full of cries- rough wailings of a child left in the
    cold.
A cold you could not predict.

Dear momma, dear papa,
Did you abort it or did you keep it?
Was it worth it?

Heaven's stars,
Do you mock thee for seeing
The sunrise once more?

For the sun spends the day dancing alone.
While the night sky–
Although vast–
Spends the night wanting thee to atone.

Lone survivor,
In return for leaving them behind they all mock thee from the
very sky thee sees til dawn.

Haunted by their faces,
You try to join them.

- *To my brother in arms, thank you for your service
  within the Dark Horse Battalion. Thank you for
  continuing and inspiring me to enlist.*

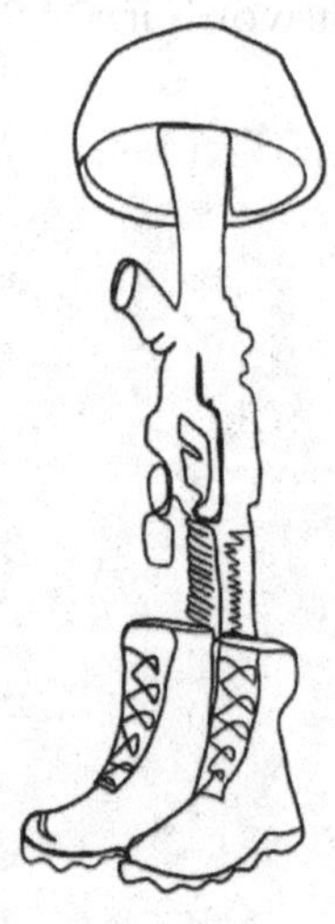

Remember.

You can't change your sins of the past...

But–

Everything you do from here onward can't be erased either.

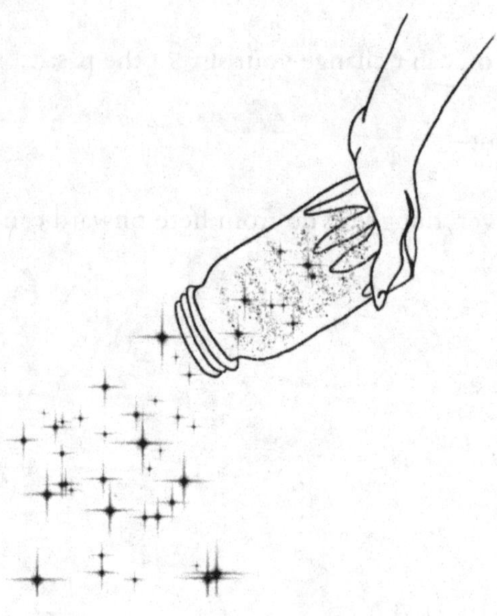

This very night sky is shared by the miles apart
Twinkling stars that whisper "I miss you." amongst the dark.

Darling, do you look up and think of me as I do you?
Is it love when one's heart both ache
And glows recalling memories of you?
Is it?

The night sky closes the distance for two who are miles apart.
Twinkling stars that say "I once saw them with you."

Twinkling stars that promise I'll see them again with you.

A day where steady hearts waver-
While loving hearts savor
The sweet intoxication known as infatuation.

Spend your money on me,
Waste every penny knowing
I won't be here tomorrow.

Spend some time with you,
Accept you are not him,
And I'm searching for someone to borrow.

A night where broken hearts now shatter-
Because he does not trust her,
Nor her sweet lies of borrowed time.

Perhaps you'll never heal.

That's okay.

I'll grow and be a new kind of strong.

-   *A conversation within my inner thoughts*

The kind of girl that starts
Wildfires because she wanted to feel warmth in her chest.

She was something like a flame
A light for those around her, but painful to touch.

The kind of girl to have no regrets
But will forever burn for the scars on her back and the sins in
her pocket.

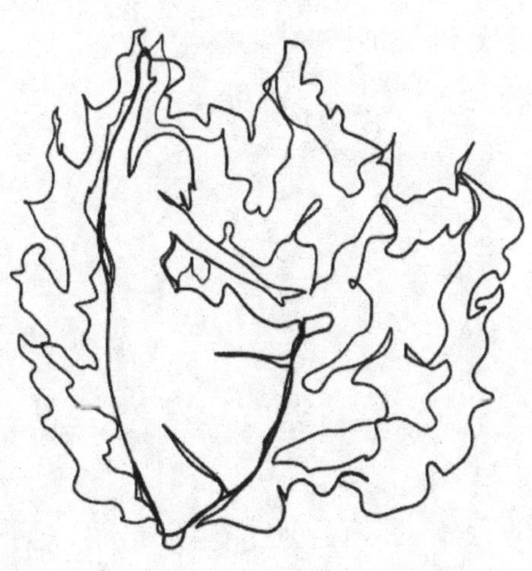

A broken heart is all you need
To come and join me in the sea…

"Come and join me in the ocean
Made of salty tears and bitter poison.

Listen to my siren's song.
The sound of angel's voices.
Made of tainted choices.

Dance to the crashing waves
Falling deeper into the ocean
Forgetting all commotion."

The only guarantee to lose your pain
Is to sing the song of the siren.

A withering rose says
"I love you."
Although I'm a bit damaged.

It means to love another knowing
The imperfections of living life day to day.

It whispers
"I am a survivor."
With black edges and falling thorns.

A withering rose says
"Love me."
For I have lived and wished to be put to rest.

Sweetheart, I thank you for the
Words you speak, soft and kind.
Only you can make my heart flutter
Remembering our precious memories.
Don't ever question your place
So that we may continue happily together.

The witch bent down to

Gaze at the child before her.

"If you're anything like me,
You will forever be alone."

The lizard on her shoulder
Bowed its head before exploding.

Perhaps the pain of going
Unnoticed was too overwhelming.
Thought the child.

"No ma'am. Now you are like me."

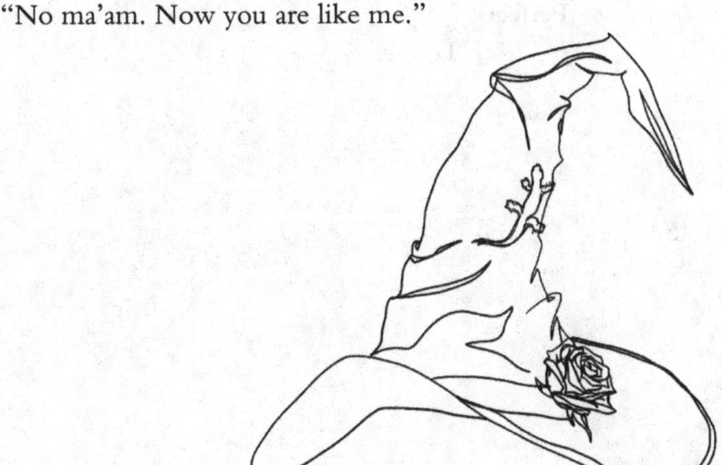

"I promise not to catch feelings."

The following are rules that are somewhat true…
A little list from me to you.

1. Promises are not to be broken
2. I'll never say, "I love you too"
3. Remember that we are both imperfect

Looking now
It seems I've fallen.
All I say is
"I love you too."
I can't recall a time you
Didn't seem
        Perfect
          To me.

Time is irrelevant to the heart

Just because you KISSED me
Doesn't mean you OWN me

You think you can FIX me
I promise you'll never CONTROL me

And even after all that's happened,
Not once did you
Doubt my intentions.
Remember me for how I loved you
Even though it's true I broke you

Sometimes people take "no"
As a
"Just ask again"

Time will pass indefinitely.

Every song that plays

Every glance exchanged

Every hour together...

We are definite.

Even though I may never see you again,

I'll hold you in my memories.

Although we made the promise as pretend...

It's something that I'll always keep

A water drop stops mid-air .
Perhaps we should have left her there.
A recollection of all she was
We think the girl had died because-

She wished for all of time to stop,
Then wished for her precious clock to drop.
Now it's broken on the floor,
We can't get the girl behind the door.
Hours pass before the medics came
Her mind of a maze now seemed tamed.

Or empty.

Vegetable girl

Vegetable girl

You've been jinxed to never think.

I hate moving to new places

With someone I know.

All these new faces

Steal the person I know.

Walls of glass now teeter-tot
Fill my glass with specs of blood.
Came close to seeing heaven's gate
But her reflection said,
"This is not your fate."

This feeling
It's nostalgic.
A feeling I thought was lost to me.
It's something like
"I want to know you."
The kind of thing
That keeps me near you.
But I know my heart
And I know my habits.
This feeling is better lost to me.
It's nostalgic.
Let's keep it that way

In my head I heard a whisper
This feeling came and kind of hit her.
Up til now I've only known numb
To do what's best, I'll just play dumb.
If I said it, would you run?
The words "I love you." Left my tongue.
Divert my gaze from anticipation
I know your answer from the hesitation.

I'm not me when I'm near you.

Or maybe

I'm only me when I'm with you.

And that scares me.

Speak.
A silent voice is a silenced noise.
One that says the cause isn't worthy.

Look.
It's uncomfortable to glare at the ugly,
But shut eyes can't see possibilities of redemption.

Stand.
Watching from a distance should
inspire you to run into the crossfire.

And if you fall.
You become a pillar to build upon once more.

Some things are better left unsaid.

My reasons being I couldn't sleep in bed.

It's hard to think you would try to tread

The wandering thoughts running through my head.

I really like the word "don't"

It dares me to.

To stand.
To fight.
To live.

It's the kind of thing
Where hidden glances are exchanged.
It makes me think
I wonder if he feels the same.
It's the feeling of
Wanting to be with you.
It's knowing that
When it's over, I'm going to miss you.

I'm
    Selfish
        &
           You're
              Greedy.

I wanted you all to myself…
You wanted more than one love

Everyone knows of you,
But how many see you?

It's a question that often crosses my mind.
At what point did you become so intriguing?
I ask, but I know.

It was your gaze–
Full of wondrous excitement and lust.
The way you stood–
Full of pride mixed with a sense of danger.
The quirks in your smile–
A mischievous warning masked by an innocent grin.

Everyone knows of you,
But I'd like to see you.

I'm broken.

I've found some pieces
Laying around,

But I'll never be whole-
Because you took some with you.

Berry.

A name so sweet
Leaves
The most bitter taste
That runs down
To my gut.

She's so empty,
She feels everything.
Enough to remember
Enough to regret.

Blurry faces whisper,
"Come find me"
Silhouettes reenact scenes long forgotten.

I don't remember for a reason
But I'd like to know the reason
Until I know the reason
I'd like to forget the reason
Until I forget again.

End it before too much time is wasted.
I say wasted because after any heartbreak- the memories burn…
Discard them.

Forget the days of holding hands and
Stealing kisses walking down the lane.

Forget the nights of tight embraces and
Drowsy whispers of "I love you"
Before the night ends.

Forget the reason why you fell,
And forget the eyes you once stared into because
They like to say "fuck, I missed you."

Forget the vicious fights because
They too tell you "even after that
I want to be with you."

Forget.
Because this time we didn't come
Back to one another.

This time.

This time it ends forever.

I see her traits in your eyes
Her smile a little brighter than yours.
Her gaze a bit warmer.
Perhaps because you aren't her,
And you know this,
Your heart feels a bit colder.

I'm sorry.

Because my forever love didn't last forever…
And I'm here with you.

Falling for you is like the slow
Stream of honey.

I love nothing more than
The sweet savory flavor
Of you.

Curious to know more from
The smooth words that escape
Your lips.

Cravings, the warmth of
Your skin trinkles down
My body, warm dew
Reminds me of happier
Times.

My happiest times are spent with you.

It wasn't til the tear

Trickled down my cheek,

I noticed the aching

In my chest

And how it connected to

My heart.

A flame erupts.
When you mandate me on what to do
Echoes scream "rebel!"
And I fight the urge to hurt you.
A smirk escapes.
Because I know exactly how to.

Today the soul suffocates.
Heavy breaths escape my lips
Wishing to grasp for something
That's no longer there.

Today the chest sinks into the mattress.
I bury myself into my arms
Hoping I am enough to carry the heavy
Aches that seep from my body.

Today the eyes cry.
My lips curl from bitterness,
Maybe which holds me to my bed today
Will kill me in my sleep tonight.

Waking up on the wrong side of bed
Can leave you fucked up in the head.
Maybe what whispers, "kill yourself"
Will find some time to do it for me.

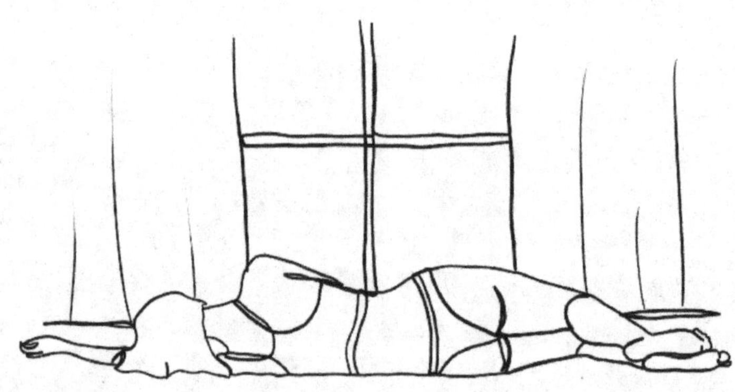

"I'll stay beside you,
Even if it's in silence."
Don't promise me better times
Or give me mini-highs that only last in the moment
Because once you leave me alone
The lows will seep back into my soul
And I'll want to die again once more.

If I were to take a couple

I heard they'll numb my body.

So that the aches stop hurting.

If I take the whole bottle

I heard they'll numb the mind.

So that the aches stop.

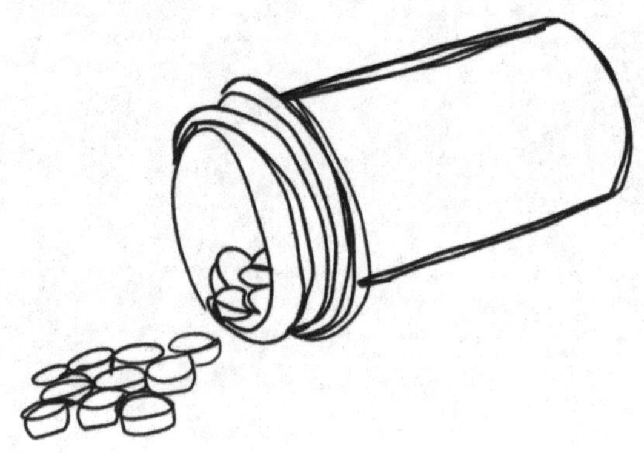

I once said,

"Yesterday's problems are to be
Left in the past
As tomorrow's problems cling to the
Necks of my future.

My everlasting soul will endure
What must be faced today."

It seems my world is crashing
And I am stuck inside.

As I was about to check on an
Old friend, a stranger interrupted
Me. She called me her new
Friend. I'll take it as a sign to let go
And move on.

Timing means everything.
In a moment of trial,

Chance called my name,
Fate showed me the road,
And I followed.

Timing means everything.

I would like to sit
Alone in silence
For there are words I cannot speak
And maybe if it's quiet
You'll hear the wails of my heart.

I would like to close my eyes
Alone beside you
For there are expressions I cannot show
And maybe if you look
You'll see the cries of my heart.

I would like to lay
Alone in my coffin.
For there are things people never notice
And maybe in my forever sleep
They'll see the signs left behind by my heart.

I'm normally detached.
I feel a type if apathy where anyone
Can say or do anything and I don't
Feel anything at all.
Until it involves you.
Then I feel everything.
I feel a type of intensity where
Anyone can say or do nothing yet
I want to react. I'm infatuated.
Practically obsessed.

I'm intoxicated with you.

I can't do anything

Because I am a jinx.

All I do is leave chaos behind me

And I don't repent.

I've embodied the word

So it hurts less when everything falls apart.

I met someone new
And he treats me better.
Don't ask me to come back
Because that girl died with you.

I don't think to say people change,
What changes is knowledge of someone.

Meeting at first
You notice what they let you see
And that sets the foundation.

As you grow less interesting to them
That's when you see their true nature.

You'll be fine.
You've lost people before.

Take it one day at a time.

I've known you for the entirety of my life
Yet it seems you of all people
Know me the least
Because I hide from you–
Because I fear to see the pain
That will surely flicker in your eyes
When you take on my burdens
And wonder why *you* failed
To protect me.
I lie because I want
To protect you,
But also because I am a coward.
Even now,
I tell the world my stories
While taking on a pen name
So that you never know–
I need my mommy and daddy
To never know…
The last of what holds me together
Is your pride in raising me *right*,
Raising a strong, willful, happy baby girl.

I love you

Yours truly,
Calypso

Acknowledgements

Bruce Brown
Damarius Fletcher
Jason Scott
Melissa Alcantar
Oscar Guillen
Scott Kwiatkowski
Subin Skariah
Zoe Gleba

Thank you to the Marines who gave me the strength to overcome my fears and surpass my limitations. Thank you to my friends and mentors for listening, supporting, and helping me during my recovery.

Enne is an author, poet, and artist; she enjoys being hands-on in her projects and even designed the cover for *Convalesce*. She is a full-time student working to obtain her BA in Business Administration while serving as an Active Duty Marine. She chooses to remain anonymous until the end of her active service in the United States Marine Corps.

www.ingramcontent.com/pod-product-compliance
Lightning Source LLC
Chambersburg PA
CBHW011934050726
47590CB00011B/3279